The Ruston Peach

Family

Stories from the Mitcham Farm

Ron Coody

CONTENTS

ACKNOWLEDGMENTS

After Joe and Cynthia Mitcham inherited their parents' farm house they decided to open it for missionaries to use when staying in the US. Our family benefitted from their warm hospitality after working 20 years in Central Asia. Deep in the heart of Kazakhstan we had a few apricot and apple trees, so we had a little experience with growing fruit. Living on the Mitcham orchard opened our eyes to a different world. I want to thank the Mitcham family for opening their heart and home in sharing these stories. Many people enjoyed Mitcham peaches for over half a century. We all owe them our gratitude.

1

No Free Peach

The new wife of Joe Mitcham Jr. returned home to the peach orchard. She had worked hard all day at her nursing job. It was the late 1970s and the Mitcham peach orchard was operating at full tilt. Dozens of college kids manned the big peach shed. Many other community folks from all walks of life worked in the fields picking and sorting, packing and selling. Cynthia walked to the sales area thinking she would get exercise in the sun. The summer sun beat down and she found herself having to stand in line with many others to get some peaches. All she wanted was two peaches just to refresh herself. She looked for her husband Joe but he was extremely busy with the operations, so she decided to wait for his break to talk. When her turn came, a regular worker at the shed, Coach "Dusty" Rhodes, would not give her a peach because she had no money with her. He said no one gets a peach without paying and that she must be crazy to think she would get one for free. She explained that she had no money with her. "Well, can I talk to Joe?" she said.

Just then Mr. J.E. Mitcham walked up. In the hot sunshine the long line of customers exchanged suspicious glances at this delay. He said that no, she could not talk to Joe. Not easily put off, the newest member of the peach family decided to stay longer and wait for her husband. But when Joe finally had a break he stayed under the shed checking on his large team of sorters and packers, many of whom were teenage and college girls, who enjoyed the attention of the nice looking, young junior Mitcham.

Cynthia watched from a distance, feeling tired. All she wanted was a peach. She hadn't seen Joe Jr. for a week because he had been running the sprinkler system night and day. Exasperated, she left the shed and walked down the road to check her mailbox. Just then the mail carrier pulled up. He looked at her and said menacingly, "You know it's a federal offense to get in a mailbox that's not your own?" She looked around. Was he talking to her? She thought it was apparent that she looked like a wife, very professional looking, not some random teenager who was stalking Joe. She did not move from the mailbox.

He warned her again. "I'm going down to report you to the police."

She replied, "I don't think so."

"But this is not your mailbox."

"Yes, it is," she insisted. "I'm Mrs. Joe Mitcham."

He insisted. "It's not your mail box."

She explained that it was in fact hers.

He argued. "This is Mr. Joe Mitcham Jr.'s"

"Well, I'm Mrs. Joe Mitcham."

He said, "No you're not, Joe's not married.

Trying to stay calm, she answered, "Yes he is, he's been married a year."

The man shifted uneasily and asked if she would not happen to be a certain Mrs. Cynthia G. Mitcham. She said that yes, that was her professional name, the way that she signed it in her nursing job.

He said, "I've been sending all your mail back."

She answered that she was well aware of that and she knew that he had sent back her state board nurses license.

She left their mail box and walked beyond it, down in the ditch up to the nearest peach tree. Two peaches hung within reach, beautiful to sight and pleasant to touch. Like Eve in the garden she pulled the fruit from the tree. She did not like her peaches over ripe, but rather just firm with medium juice. Just then Two Gun Son rode up on patrol and said, "You're not supposed to be picking peaches."

Cynthia Mitcham tried to explain to the off-duty police officer. "They wouldn't let me have any up at the shed." He wanted to know who exactly she thought she was and that nobody can go into the fields and pick peaches. NOBODY. He was hired to make the rounds on it.

She said, "I just wanted a peach."

"You're going to have to give it back," he said.

Maybe the heat was getting to everyone and she insisted, "No. No, I'm not."

11

He said, "Yeaaah, you are." So right then and there he arrested her. First he took away her two peaches. Then he put her in handcuffs and put her in the back of the car. She was getting really mad.

Instead of taking her to Ruston he drove up to the peach shed. Where was J.E.? They found him and presented this freshly apprehended peach thief. He looked at his daughter-in-law of one year. Two Gun Son pulled her out of the car and stood by. A hundred curious customers suddenly lost interest in the peaches. Dozens of young girls under the shed kept packing peaches but craned their necks to watch. Mothers pulled their children up close and whispered warningly. A fly buzzed.

Did J.E. want to press charges? He felt the eyes of all of Ruston fall on him. He had been running the peach orchard for 30 years like a stern British sea captain. Could he afford a moment of weakness? He drew a breath and answered, "Yes."

Cynthia gasped and shook. All this over a peach? Yet no one was ever allowed to pick a peach. Not even J.E.'s wife Marzee. The peaches always came first. If she ever got any peaches it was with her little yellow bucket. She gathered them from under the tree on the ground and they were bird-pecked.

Still pleading her case, Cynthia pleaded to see Joe. Calling her parents would not have helped. If she ever called them the only thing her mother would say was, "be nice to Joe."

It was probably a close friend of the Mitcham family, Chief Osburn who called Joe to come out. Feeling the stares of all the customers and workers, he got up his courage to approach his dad. They talked quietly. Joe urged him to not press charges. J.E. finally agreed but repeated that Cynthia needed to always abide by the orchard rules and could never pick a peach.

In a last attempted protest, she said that she tried to get a peach but no one would give her one so she had to go pick one herself. By then she did not want to defend herself. Let all the customers and workers think what they would. Still standing there in handcuffs she felt that she was right and God knew she was right.

Two Gun Son got the nod from J.E. and removed the handcuffs. Cynthia walked home empty handed. The humiliated new bride, whether she knew it then or not, had helped the Mitcham family put the fear of God into another generation of peach lovers.

Nobody really gets a free peach, not even the peach family. But they're always worth the price.

2

The Roots

"These peach cobblers just aren't quite as good as the ones I remember as a child." J.E. said to everyone seated at the dinner table. He always sat at the head of the table. Behind him was a large window looking out into the backyard with a massive old pecan tree. The founder of the feast thoughtfully took another bite of the delicious peach cobbler.

Marzee knew all about his love of sweets and perfectionism. She was a little woman, much shorter than J.E., but could move quickly around the kitchen and the orchard. She looked over at him with her pretty dark brown eyes and replied with a wry smile, "I use margarine and your mother used real butter."

"Nothing makes good peach cobbler like real butter," he answered. The lack of real butter did not slow J.E. nor anyone else from enjoying the fruit of their labor. The sweet aroma of Mitcham peaches filled their modest farm house that stood in the middle of the well-known orchard. This wasn't the first peach cobbler Marzee had crafted and –in spite of the margarine – it would not be the last one the Mitcham family would enjoy together.

J.E Mitcham knew about lots more than just what makes a good peach cobbler. He was a polymath; someone possessing an amazing command of subjects and skills developed and pursued over a lifetime. He studied music, earning a distance learning degree from the Vandercook School of Music in Chicago. He taught a wide range of subjects in public school, from band to science and math. His contributions to Ruston, Lincoln Parish and Louisiana through service on boards and committees was extraordinary. Before finally retiring from formal employment, J.E. had helped shape the identity of Ruston through his relationships with generations of students, friends and co-workers.

J.E. came from the small village of Summerfield, north of Ruston. For a small corner of Louisiana, the region produced a large number of highly successful people. From the Haley family, two became renowned anesthesiologists and another a college math professor. Karl Malone is another Summerfield name known around the world. The Robertsons of Duck Dynasty lived nearby in the Louisiana highlands.

Summerfield folks, like many living between the Red and Mississippi Rivers, tended to lean away from urbanization. Hunters, trappers, homesteaders and farmers, they moved into the piney hills and river bottoms willing to put up with redbugs and ground rattlers for the sake of building an independent life.

Growing up in Summerfield, J.E. got a taste of outdoor and organic life. He never gave it up. With the strong will of a mighty sea captain—but one who would never use foul language or drink rum—he conquered the rolling fields of 340 acres bringing delight and summer fun to Lincoln Parish and beyond.

This dream of producing peaches apparently did not arise on an impulse when he and Marzee contemplated purchasing land near Ruston. As a hard-working teen J.E. raised peach trees on his parents' farm in Summerfield. His vivacious mother Valarie and quiet father Arnold encouraged his interest in farming. They could also see his wide range of skills and abilities and urged him to get his degree from Louisiana Tech University.

A generous place, Tech not only gave J.E. a degree in music, it introduced him to Marzee, who was taking general studies. With J.E. at 21 years old and Marzee a youthful 19, they discovered that their friendly interest in one another would give way to courtship and then marriage.

Coming out of the Great Depression and struggling with minimal cash as college students, neither they nor their families could afford an elaborate wedding and honeymoon. Asking around, they heard that an evangelist was holding revival services at a Baptist Church. Someone offered them a ride into the country. They traveled to the meetings and took the rather unusual step of taking their wedding vows before the evangelist after the evening meeting was over. It wasn't an elopement, but simply the best they could do under the circumstances.

Marzee's family ran a small country store in Castor, Louisiana, so they were somewhat better off than the Mitchams in Summerfield. If they really needed something to eat or for the house, they could get what they needed from the store. Later in life she would reminisce about Christmas time during the depression. The kids would get a stocking full of nuts and an orange. One time she got a purse and pen which was a pretty good haul during the Great Depression. She ate the orange on Christmas Day.

J.E. and Marzee considered their honeymoon options. Where could they go with their tiny budget? Was there someplace scenic, exotic? Maybe even a trip to a new place outside of North Louisiana? What made better sense than Hot Springs, Arkansas? Known for its thermal waters, it was a real tourist spot close enough to Ruston they could reach with their old car. Marzee's parents let the newlyweds pack their car with groceries from the family market, enough to feed them the whole six days.

In Hot Springs the young Mitchams enjoyed themselves, to the point of splurging on a nickel ice cream cone. Maybe it was love, maybe it was Arkansas ice cream or maybe it was hot weather, but something about that cone was so special that they often retold their children and grandchildren about that nickel cone for the rest of their married days.

After six days in their Hot Springs hotel, the Mitchams learned they could have a seventh day compliments of the management. To their immense disappointment, they could not call their parents to inform them they were staying an extra day since no one had a telephone at home. They were concerned if they did not come back on the sixth day as planned, their folks would start to worry too much that something bad had happened. Along with the story of the amazing nickel ice cream cone, they would often talk about how sorry they were that they did not get to take that free seventh day and night. Even in old age, when they could travel anywhere they desired, they never completely got over that lost honeymoon day.

J.E. left Tech with a degree in music and headed southeast with his new wife to Vidalia on the Mississippi river, just across from Natchez. Agriculture may not have been the first thing on his mind as a new husband and new band director, but the fabulously rich cotton fields of the lower Mississippi Delta could not have escaped his notice. Engineers were putting up a soaring new bridge across the Mississippi River that would soon make the old southern plantations of Natchez accessible, just another reminder of the fertile farmlands of the area. For the grand opening of the Vidalia-Natchez Bridge, J.E. had the rare privilege of leading his marching band across the muddy waters. Looking westward from the middle of the high span he could see for miles into his lush home state.

While World War 2 took millions of men and woman away from home, it also required millions more to stay behind in support roles. J.E.'s brother went into the military but the government offered J.E. the somewhat ho-hum option of staying on the farm to raise potatoes. The Mitchams packed up their sparse household and went back north. They settled into the farm life again and put the music on hold, except for church meetings. The potato farming helped prepare him for future days, when his work in the Louisiana fields would not be so mundane.

With victory in WW2, America moved suddenly and dramatically into a period of euphoric growth. No area of life went untouched by the new optimism of the post-war period. The genius and personal energy of J.E. could not just sit contentedly on a potato farm in Summerfield. He needed a place where his dreams could stretch out and grow and flourish. But his dreams encompassed a wide range of fields, not just the farming kind. He enjoyed teaching music and other subjects. He enjoyed investing in young people, helping students grasp a new mathematical concept or learn a new grammar rule so they could express themselves more clearly. The schoolhouse called out to him.

Still, those farm lands had learned how to call his name. Okay, maybe potatoes were not the most exciting things to grow. But they put a solid meal on the table and since he had lived through the Great Depression and WW2 he certainly would not want to downplay the importance of having a square meal. A visionary, he could see that America was entering a period of optimism and plenty. People would soon not only be concerned about getting enough food on the table for supper but might even think about luxuries like dessert...like a peach cobbler.

The Mitchams looked at their options. Where could they work as teachers and also pursue their dreams for growing delicious fruit on a large scale? Perhaps near Ruston? They were Tech grads and knew the area. Another peach grower, Mr. Owens had a large peach orchard north of Ruston in the community of Hico. Apparently the iron-rich red hills of Lincoln Parish supported the growth of decent peaches. It was something worth considering.

In 1946 the Mitchams moved to Ruston when the high school hired J.E. as their band director. He was pleased to have landed a job in such a reputable school system also near his alma mater and not far from his hometown. Marzee also got a job teaching. Having good teaching jobs was a blessing, but something else added a special luster to their lives. Working in Ruston put the Mitchams near an incredible opportunity.

Just a few miles west of Ruston and the older community of Vienna, the old Garr cotton plantation went on the market. Many years earlier cotton was the traditional cash crop of the area. Everybody did cotton. When the railroad first came through Ruston in the post-Civil War days people started shipping out cotton. But the cotton days were passing away. There was a little peach orchard in Vienna in the 1920s. J.E.'s ancestors had migrated from the Georgia area, so perhaps some of them from the east had passed down the idea of peach orchards.

Whatever the reason, J.E. wanted to plant peaches outside of Ruston. With the business proposal in mind, he inquired about the Garr property. What a price! The rolling highland was for sale at $36.00 an acre! From the Mitcham's point of view, it was a lot of money. One acre of land was 720 times the cost of that tasty ice cream cone they bought in Hot Springs in their once-in-a-lifetime honeymoon splurge. Furthermore, they weren't looking at 1 acre but 300. It was a mind-boggling purchase and they were two relatively poor schoolteachers who had just come from a small potato farm. Neither were they the type to take out a lot of loans. They scrimped and saved and never splurged.

But their vision for a beautiful orchard proved greater than worries about a big loan. They took the loan and bought the 300 acres for $10,800. They wanted to purchase the whole 500 acres plantation, but the bank would not give these young school teachers a loan that big. Today one acre of similar land would cost $9,000. It is amazing to imagine how they got an old plantation for so little by today's standards, but more amazing to see how they would transform it.

3

The Fruit

The peach is the star of this story. The reddish-yellow fruit seems to blush after a brief kiss with the sun. It gives humans a unique set of sensations with its size, color, firmness, flavor and texture. Lincoln Parish peach growers such as the Mitchams and their contemporaries the Owens, Summeralls, Hollises, Stormants, Carroways, Lawrences and others did not invent the peach. The peach stands on its own. Of course it has benefitted from millennia of human cultivation. But it would be arrogant to forget that while humanity may be clever enough to build an Apple computer, it could never make a peach.

Who could think of the weirdly bothersome peach fuzz that feels like a sixteen-year-old's soft cheek? How could anyone ever capture the soft glow of the setting sun in the yellow peach peeling? How could that reddish blush hinting of a stolen kiss on a sultry summer night be the product of a test tube? Maybe it is silly to say, but is there anything quite so deliciously alluring than a peach?

As a teenage boy on his parents' Louisiana farm, J.E. made a very important friendship. Planting a few peach trees, perhaps from some pits left over from an afternoon snack, he started a friendship with a fruit that would give back to him many times over. He could not have known then, but his peaches would travel the United States. Governors would enjoy their peachiness and Presidents Nixon, Reagan, Bush and Clinton would eventually get in on the taste too.

Prunis persica. The peach comes in all sizes, shapes and colors, except maybe a black, square block. Some stay tiny and others grow to over a pound. There are bright red varieties and bright yellow ones. The level of juice in a single peach can get high enough to fill a large cup. In the world's northern hemisphere the peach flourishes under clear skies and bright, warm sunshine.

Turning back time, the search for the first cultivated peaches leads on a wilderness trek. Peaches in the New World came over from Europe with Spanish missionaries. They introduced the 'queen of fruits' to Native Americans in the Southwest. American soil liked the peach tree and within a few generations peaches had spread all over the country, even without the help of a folk hero like Johnny Appleseed. Many of these early American peaches matured late and had firm, red flesh. Today these are still called Indian peaches. Arkansas was one territory known as early as the 1800s for growing many of these.

Following the peach trail leads across the Atlantic to Europe. Monasteries grew peaches for centuries across southern Europe. The Romans brought peaches to England, but when their empire fell, peaches did not survive in the unfamiliar climate. Greece had peaches as early as 322 B.C. The peach came to Europe compliments of Alexander the Great. In between conquering Asia, he and his hungry hordes probably feasted on peaches in Persia. The Latin name *perisca* is a case of mistaken identity. The Europeans traced the fruit to Persia, but the trail actually goes back deeper into the mysterious land of the Far East.

The trek now turns northeastward from Persia into the remote and wild country of Turkistan (now Kazakhstan and western China). The peach grows well in Central Asia, but the trail to the original peach goes along the same paths as the Silk Road. Chinese and other Asian merchants probably discarded peach pits on their business trips. They got the peaches from an area near the city of Xian deep in the heart of China.

Xian is China's version of St. Louis. Both cities marked the gateway to their country's West. For the peach to make its entry into the global market, Xian provided the perfect launching pad. Wild peaches grew in the forests and mountains of the Xian region. Chinese farmers cultivated this fruit many years ago during the Shou Dynasty 1000 years before Christ. Xian proved a reliable gateway. The peach spread westward from the Chinese heartland until it brought pleasure to lovers of fresh fruit and pies and pastries around the world.

Bananas and apples have the advantage of long shelf life, but take that away and the peach is clearly superior. Ever had a juicy banana? If you did it was probably rotten. Apple cobbler? No thanks. How about fresh apple ice cream? Umm…Nah.

There's tons of good stuff behind the peach's pretty face. Calcium and potassium strengthen the boney frame. Other minerals and vitamins help fight cancer and improve diabetes, heart health and eyesight. It has high fiber content for good digestion. The peach brings sparkle and energy to people. Who better would know this than the first Chinese farmers that domesticated the peach? Maybe that is why in China the peach tree became a symbol of longevity and a blessed life.

Starting a new family and moving into Ruston after a devastating world war; that was exactly what J.E. and Marzee Mitcham wished for themselves and others. In 1946 with 300 acres stretching to the horizon, the Mitchams began digging the groundwork for an orchard of longevity and a blessed life.

4

Hog Pens and Hot Sun

John Albert Hunter kept his hogs downhill from the orchard close to where Marzee would later build her garden house. He was the orchard foreman who came from Summerfield with J.E. A right-hand-man and close friend, John Albert worked alongside J.E. to get the peach orchard moving in the 1940s and 50s. With nine kids he needed those hogs. And if anybody could help welcome the Mitcham's future children and their spouses into the Peach family, it was John Albert. His friendly and easy demeanor gave a relaxed feel to the whole operation.

From the very beginning 300 acres presented far more work than a single man could ever hope to manage. So J.E. regularly hired other workers. In the late spring when the Louisiana sun got hotter the numbers of workers got larger and larger. Some drove tractors and sprayed. Trimmers and pruners knocked blooms off the tree to increase production. Pickers flooded in to harvest the fruit. The peach orchard would quickly grow in size and production in those early days requiring lots of skills and laborers. At the peak they had 35 workers in the peach shed and 35 or more in the fields.

Terracing the soil was a common farming practice in the Louisiana hilly areas. The terraces insured gradual flow of rain water instead of fast runoff. One day J.E. was chatting about farming with his neighbor Mr. Wilder whose land adjoined the orchard to the south. He and J.E. were good friends and he worked for the Soil Conservation Service. J.E. was good at making terraces, so the Soil Conversation Service offered a chance to make some extra income around the area.   For a nickel a foot J.E. brought out his special plow and tractor and pulled up tons of red dirt. It was not easy money. It took 27 rounds with a plow and a blade to build the terrace. The plow would break up the soil and the blade would roll the soil up into a hill.

J.E. was an outstanding innovator. A childhood prank gives a little insight into this ability. When he was about 12 years old he patiently taught his younger sister Helen to memorize some Bible verses written on cards. She was eight years younger than him. When she was about four years old he took her to the school and told the teacher she knew how to read. He would have her hold the cards and 'read' the bible verse.

Perfectionism made J.E. keep some farm tasks to himself. Years before their first child arrived, he learned how to baby each peach sapling and intimately knew each tree. His pruning innovations gave the Mitcham orchard a large advantage in

pro

duction. He started with the small tree, systematically pruning it so it always had three main scaffolds and again six main branches as the tree grew outwards and upwards. He weighted the tree branches to get the correct angle and maximize the amount of sun getting into the tree, which in turn maximized the fruit.

This pattern of pruning and innovation never really changed for the next 60 years. Until he was 90 Mr. Mitcham worked the fields, gently pruning the trees. At the height of the orchard he would oversee 34,000 trees, roughly 100 per acre. Like gnarly old tree Ents, each tree had a unique personality, thanks to his creative touch with pruning and sculpting the trees.

He also worked with an LSU research station in Calhoun, experimenting with the branches and farming techniques. J.E. would go on to become a popular presenter at peach conferences in Texas, Alabama, Georgia and South Carolina, making

Ruston and Mitcham orchard well-known across the South.

5

Making a Name

While Mr. Mitcham doted the peach saplings, Marzee kept busy around the new farm and with her teaching job in Ruston. Getting there proved challenging on the dirt road leading off the farm to Cooktown Road. At some point early in the orchard's history she insisted to her husband that they buy a house in Ruston or buy a plot of land and build a house. She was tired of living out in the country. The dirt road was a nuisance, especially with all the rain in Louisiana. A muddy road did not quite fit life in the 1950s for a young professional. It seemed funny that she would have cared about the dirt road since she was from Castor, Louisiana in the middle of nowhere.

But maybe she did not want to live in the middle of nowhere any more. J.E. agreed to look and they found a place near Cook Baptist Church off Cooktown. The Mitcham Orchard story might have looked a lot different except that Lincoln Parish paved the road and she decided she could stay on the farm.

In the early days everyone called Mr. Mitcham simply "Mitcham" and later he became known as J.E. or Edward. Marzee called him 'Mr. J.E.', saying things like, "Mr. J.E., have you had enough dinner, are you ready for dessert?" Her real first name was Willie, but she hated that name and never used it.

The peach orchard grew, John Albert's family grew, the hog pen grew and the Mitcham family grew, though not all at the same pace. Marzee got pregnant with their first child. She carried the baby nine months but he was still-born. They had a funeral for baby Arnold, named after J.E.'s father. The loss of their firstborn affected them deeply and they did not talk about him for years. When Joe Jr. and Cynthia had their second daughter Sarah, Mr. J.E. surprisingly would not come to the hospital. Touched by the birth of his fourth grandchild, he cried and said, "She looks just like Arnold."

In 1951 Mr. Mitcham put himself into helping plan the first Ruston Peach Festival. He was president of the Louisiana Fruit Growers Association and worked with Walter Smith, chairman of the Peach Festival. It was a gala event of a massive scale. Peach decorations covered the city of Ruston. The Dixie Gem peach, a well-known variety at the time, inspired the Dixie Gem pageant. Judges selected the peach festival queen from the prettiest girls who promoted the prettiest peaches. Ann Colvin of Bernice got the honors of Queen Dixie Gem, presented to her by Sen.

Dudley Le Blanc. Lou Ellen Stevens became the first Princess Peach, long before the Nintendo Mario game came up with its fictional damsel in distress. The Louisiana Cajun celebrity Justin Wilson made crowds hoot at the Louisiana Tech Howard auditorium and he emceed the entire event.

The Ruston Peach Festival was such a huge success in the early 1950s that it made Mr. Mitcham, already a hard worker, feel more responsible than ever. *The Ruston Daily Leader* wrote in 1951, "We believe we can consider the initial effort a success. It was an extremely hard job put over by a small group of men (and women), but they did it and our whole area will rise in importance. This (Ruston) will be the new festival city, the new peach market of the south, and from it we will all benefit."[1] So it did. In 1953 Queen Dixie Gem III, Dorothy Ella Goff, presented a box of Ruston peaches to Vice President Richard Nixon. The Louisiana peach festival gave the growers a boost

---

[1] http://www.louisianapeachfestival.org/PeachHistory.html

beyond anything they dreamed and took the Mitcham orchard another step closer to a near celebrity status.

6

Joe's Daily Diary

1955 literally dumped a cold blanket over the whole affair. A late freeze killed the spring blossoms, destroying the crop. It disrupted the momentum of the Peach Festival but the organizers kept the show going by shipping in peaches from other states.

Through this period the Mitchams celebrated at home with the births of their children Jan and Joe Jr. They could easily remember the year of the big 1955 freeze because it was the year Joe came. Marzee stayed busy with the babies while Mr. Mitcham continued his leadership in the Louisiana Fruit Growers Association and the Peach Festival.

There was still time for recreation and social life. J.E. was a good shot with a gun and could hunt well. It was a skill he probably picked up by necessity during the Great Depression when wild game was abundant and jobs not. The family kept J.E.'s old gun that he used after he died. He taught Joe Jr. at a young age to hunt and fish. They kept hunting dogs when he was little and father and son spent many days enjoying the outdoors.

J.E. and Marzee were dedicated Christians and members of Temple Baptist Church in Ruston. J.E. kept a Bible next to his favorite chair and made a habit of going to church. A band director and highly trained musician, he enjoyed singing in the church choir. Other choir members would often smile when he corrected the choir director, usually about something to do with the rhythm of the music. He helped out by teaching other choir members their parts when they could not learn the music. In later years he would stop Joe Jr. in mid-song and say, "Joe you've got that rhythm wrong."

Teaching pervaded everything about the Mitchams. Jan and Joe grew up having to use good grammar or else one or both of their parents would correct them. The Mitchams would correct anyone who walked in the door. They never thought they were insulting the person, though it may have embarrassed folks sometimes. They kept a high standard in everything for themselves and everyone around them.

In 1964 J.E. and Marzee moved from next to the peach shed into their new farm house across the street. It served them well for the rest of their lives. The house stood on high ground and was the site of the dairy during the Garr plantation days. Two sentinels stood in the front yard. One was a massive cedar tree, easily large enough to compete for one of the South's largest, and the other a sprawling magnolia. The Mitchams built the house with brick dappled in shades of red, white and gray, making the place blend seamlessly with the surrounding iron hills and peach blossoms. Several pecan trees, oaks and pines made up a large wooded area behind the house, enticing deer and other woodland creatures to visit, as though the peaches were not already a powerful temptation.

With both parents regularly correcting grammar and teaching in school, it must have been a natural thing for Joe Jr. to get inspired to keep a diary when he was around 12 years old. For the most part it read like an appointment book with a few lines of commentary every day. Most of it contained run-of-the-mill information like, "I did my homework, watched some TV and went to bed." Then again every once in a while he wrote something a little more interesting such as, "today was my birthday and I got a knife and a dollar." One day in particular however records what could have become a catastrophic day in the history of the orchard. He wrote, "I did my homework, watched some TV and then caught the yard on fire with a magnifying glass and almost burned down the house." He went on to write that he did not get in trouble.

While the acre of grass in the farm yard still smoldered, Joe Jr.'s parents calmly discussed with him the danger of starting a fire with a magnifying glass and then let him go to bed. They did not punish him or scold him, but allowed him to learn from his mistake, knowing that he would not do it again.

This near tragedy revealed something interesting about the peach family. Mr. Mitcham was not known as a particularly affectionate person. Like the old British sea captain, he could be stern and strong, driving his crew forward toward a goal. Yet as far as discipline in the home, he believed a parent should never strike a child; though he might take a paddle to boys in school. Joe never got a spanking. Mrs. Mitcham may have used peach switch on him for something on one occasion, but his daddy never did.

7

The Orchard Grows

Just being a small railroad town did not put Ruston on the map, but Louisiana Tech University and the Peach Festival came to the rescue. The Mitcham name became well known in the town and at the campus. Working on the Mitcham orchard during peak summer season supplemented countless college students. They graded and packed and sorted and shipped. The Mitcham orchard became one of the chief local employers of college kids during the 1960s and 70s.

Old-fashioned in attitudes toward gender roles, Mr. Mitcham expected only his son Joe Jr. to work on the orchard. Jan helped her mother in the home. While still a small boy, Joe Jr. and the Mitchams' well-loved mule Dan Tucker pitched in. They raised corn and 200 head of cattle. One year they raised 120 acres of purple hull peas. Another year they planted six acres of pole beans and had to comb the woods for hundreds of cut bean poles. Mr. Mitcham planted two acres in tomatoes one year. They did other farming here and there, but the peaches were always the most profitable.

Joe stayed on call day and night. In the summer, skunks would get into the old irrigation pipes and block them up. Sometimes these smelly squatters came out, covering Joe with their fragrance. He always had to run the irrigation shifts at night so he never slept a full 8 hours; farm work was 24/7. When Two Gun Son was not patrolling the orchard, Joe had to run the rounds for people stealing peaches. Mr. Mitcham did not care too much for dogs, so there were no watch dogs.

Theft was an occasional problem. At one of the orchards two miles down the road they had a booming cannon to scare off the deer and crows. Deer, squirrels, coons and foxes all like to eat peaches. Squirrels mostly eat them when they get ripe. The cannon worked with a propane burst and was very loud. One morning Joe found a nice sports bag about half full of peaches in the orchard near the cannon. Examining the bag, he figured the cannon went off and the thief just dropped the bag and ran. Hopefully that was all he lost in fright!

On another occasion in later years, he and Cynthia were driving on a Sunday morning and came upon a girl dressed in a moo-moo climbing the fence. She had her dress pulled up full of peaches. Over the years people have sheepishly approached Joe and Cynthia to confess. "Oh yeah, when we were in college we came and got some peaches." The Mitchams did not put up 'no stealing' signs, Joe always viewed it as common sense. After all, taking a peach off the orchard is no different than shoplifting. And there is no free peach.

After peach season the Mitchams liked to let a group come through called Gleaners. There were always a few peaches left over after harvest. They did not want these to uselessly rot, so certain local folks came through who gleaned the peaches. They also let them come in and pick leftover blueberries.

In all the years of working the farm, they had an amazingly few number of accidents. One time a rock shot out from under a bush hog mower and hit J.E.'s friend Ollie on his knee, almost as fast a bullet. As an adult, Joe dropped a heavy staple machine on his toe and another time he fell off a deer stand that was laying on its side, breaking some bones, but thankfully the accidents were not life threatening.

J.E. put Joe behind a tractor wheel before he turned thirteen. He became skilled at driving the huge fleet of Massey Fergusons. The Mitcham Orchard operated so many Massey Ferguson tractors that in 2005 the international company featured Mitcham Orchard in their magazine with the article "When Less is More." Very complementary of the farm, they said, "While the business has changed over the years, their equipment—more than a dozen Massey Ferguson tractors—is a constant." A dealer in Monroe said that people in North Louisiana knew that their equipment was well-maintained. The resale value actually increased so that a tractor purchased for $2,800 would go for $4,000.

Joe had a practical explanation for running 18 tractors. "Most people change the pieces of equipment on the back of the tractor," he said, "but I was too lazy, instead of changing out I would just get another tractor."

8

Absolutely No Smoking!

Tractors did everything in the later days, but it all started with Mr. Mitcham, John Albert and good ole' Dan Tucker. J.E., his tall, lanky frame dressed in baggy overalls, strapped himself to the mule and walked behind the big plow. From under his straw hat he watched the red dirt break into clods and form hills where he planted the peach trees.

The tractors made the work much easier of course, and they pulled plows and mowers, trailers and sprayers. They also freed up J.E. to keep planting new seedlings and sculpting the growing trees according to his innovative experiments. Always thinking ahead, he envisioned using both technology and creative techniques to coax more, larger and tastier fruit from a single tree.

If peaches have any fault, it is the fuzz, though not a fault that cannot be forgiven...or fixed. The Mitchams' first peach processing shed had a dry defuzzer, a contraption that ran the peaches through a series of brushes. Clouds of fuzz and dust filled the air. The workers had to deal with continuous itching and breathing problems. The summer heat added to the frustration when the fuzz mixed with sweat and dirt.

In 1968 Joe's diary records another fire disaster. It was far worse than the burning grass. One night the Mitchams watched with horror as huge flames and clouds of smoke billowed up from their peach processing shed. It was not only the center of operations with the dry defuzzer, it had handcrafted tables and equipment built by their good friend and neighbor Elmer Hollis, a gentle and sweet man that everyone loved. The floors were covered in sawdust and peach fuzz, making it extremely flammable. In the loft they had stored family photos and extra furniture. The fire took everything.

After the fire J.E. and Joe became ever stricter about anyone smoking around the shed. Too many things were flammable. The guys working in the loft making boxes would sometimes sneak cigarettes. The Mitchams had a no tolerance policy and fired on the spot anyone caught smoking.

Years later Joe looked back with some regret on the tragedy yet commented that "at the time it seemed like a bad thing that the shed burned, but it was the best thing that ever happened because we built a large steel building put in some modern processing equipment."

That modern equipment included a hydro-cooler and well-designed conveyer and sorter system. Orchards in Georgia and South Carolina used hydro-coolers but the Mitchams had the only one in the Louisiana. The principle was simple. Workers dumped all the peaches into a processor that sprayed the hot fruit in deliciously cool water, making them last longer. It also washed the peaches prior to their hitting the rollers with the brushes that de-fuzzed the peaches. Next they went onto the conveyor belt where workers graded the peaches. From there it was back onto little lines that fed the peaches into various containers according to grade.

Every day it changed. One day there might be a variety that had a lot of brown spots, that is, a sort of fungus. Then there were the malformed pieces of fruit, like twin peaches, that had to be graded out.

Every piece of fruit passed through the hands of many workers. The pickers plucked each piece from a tree. Then the fruit went into the conveyor system to face a battery of graders. Passed from hand to hand, bathed and sorted and de-fuzzed and packed, each piece of fruit got special care. In a good year the Mitcham Orchard could produce up to 8 million peaches, enough for every person in Louisiana and Arkansas to have a taste of the peach's longevity and blessing.

9

Senior to Junior

Racial tensions ran high in parts of America in the early 1970s. For some reason, race relations in Ruston were not quite as bad as other places. Maybe it was due in part to its small town ways. Perhaps it stemmed from the inclusive and tolerant attitude of founder Robert Russ. Maybe it had to do with the parish fathers naming it after Abraham Lincoln. Seeing the need for stable and peaceful leadership during desegregation, the local school board asked J.E. to become a principal at Ruston Elementary School. By that time he was widely known for his fair treatment of his employees regardless of race, such as his life-long friend and colleague John Albert.

Always a willing community servant, Mr. Mitcham took the new post, but he was starting to map out his retirement from public school life. In 1970 he was principal and knew he would retire in 1973 so he managed to lease a large piece of land two miles down the road from his peach shed. Hearing loss forced him years earlier to retire from directing the bands in 1964 when the doctor told him that if he did not get out of the band room he was going to go deaf. After that he taught math and science until he became school principal. From 1973 onward the orchard reached its largest size at 340 acres. Until then Mr. Mitcham planted peaches on only 160 acres of the original 300 acres since much of the Garr plantation was low land and creek bottoms not suitable for farming.

Joe Jr. graduated in 1973 from high school. Louisiana Tech gave his folks a good education, so he thought it would work for him. But just as important as attending a good school, he needed a place close enough to the orchard for him to stay on call 24/7. During the four years of taking pre-med he lived on the farm, except for a brief stint in the Sigma Nu house next to the campus.

Mr. Mitcham leaned on Joe more and more as John Albert and he aged. No one knew the farm better than Joe except Mr. Mitcham himself and no one felt more responsible to follow his daddy's instructions and wishes. He would never have dreamed of saying 'no' to his father. Their relationship was intertwined with the peach orchard and keeping it successful through the years of drought and flood and fire and ice.

As a young man, Joe never stop working. During peak production season everyone from J.E. to the lowliest teenager got an hour lunch. J.E. loved the taste of salt on his food but also poured it on because he lost so much fluid under the hot sunshine. Father and son came to the farm house at noon each day for the lunch Marzee cooked. Then they laid down and took a 15 minute nap. They never set an alarm. Both men lost lots of weight every summer from dehydrating and hard work.

Marzee loved flowers and gardening, so they built her a prefab, A-frame house on top of the hill overlooking John Albert's old hog pen after it was out of use. The cute little house resembled something a child would draw, just a one-and-half-story A-frame house with two windows looking out on the orchard. She had a garden club and enjoyed hosting meeting with her friends. She also hosted a ladies Bible study that would come to the farm house. They enjoyed her homemade peach cake and friendship together.

While Joe studied at Tech, J.E. and Marzee decided to give him permission to move into the little garden house with two of his friends. For him it was one more step--small maybe, but important--towards independence and adult life on the orchard.

After years of farm life under the blue sky, medical exam rooms and hospitals did not appeal to Joe. As graduation approached, Joe stared briefly at the fork in his road at graduation. A medical life or back to the peach orchard? The choice wasn't so hard. He finished college and stayed at the orchard. He would leave the medical ambition with Tech, but he kept a hold of something, or rather someone he found there.

Cynthia was not a Ruston native. She was an outsider. She came to Tech and studied nursing. She and Joe met one Sunday at the altar when she welcomed Joe as a new member to Temple Baptist. Apparently she had not heard the pastor Dr. Maghee introduce Joe as a former member.

Actually to be more precise, Cynthia met Joe years earlier at a different kind of sacred place. One pleasant summer evening her mother brought her over from West Monroe to the Mitcham orchard to buy some peaches. She was only nine years old. The sun had already started to set and she met Joe in the late afternoon after all the workers were gone. Mr. Mitcham had Joe still working and cleaning up. They saw each other briefly. They did not necessarily feel any romantic spark as Cynthia watched the hard-working lad sweeping under the shed. It was not quite like they were childhood lovers but it was unusual to meet then so early and not again until they were in college together.

Cynthia had another childhood experience that prepared her in a special way to identify with the Ruston peach family. One day the Avon saleslady visited her home. Along with all her other products, she presented Cynthia and her mother a little peach cream. She wanted to buy it and was pleased when her mother gave her permission. It was a bushel of peaches, just a little basket. It was a trifle, but later in marriage she cherished it in her shadow box.

Meeting as children did not generate sparks, but college was a different matter. Joe and Cynthia dated and then got engaged.

During that time Jan Mitcham finished her master's degree and Cynthia her nursing degree. Their graduation ceremony was held in the Tech stadium, but J.E. would not let Joe go because of the work load. Jan's husband Danny fixed a large meal for everyone that night to celebrate the graduations. Rain started to pour so Tech called off the outdoor ceremony to everyone's disappointment. In those days Cynthia owned an orange VW Bug that she called Agape. She and Jan drove over to Wyly tower to pick up their diplomas, but somehow Jan got lost. Waiting for an hour, Cynthia started to panic and thought that someone had mugged Jan in the poorly lighted quadrangle. At midnight she drove back to the orchard and discovered that Danny had picked up Jan hours earlier and they were safely at home in bed. Still just engaged, she had to go to her own home after a day of unexpected difficulties.

When they started making wedding plans Cynthia's church in West Monroe started excitedly renovating the auditorium for the proposed wedding. They felt fondly toward her, even though as a teenager she and her friends had broken into the church several times. They had a good reason. She sang with a music group called the Freedom Singers and for some reason the church would not give them a key. They resorted to breaking in for their practices.

Cynthia firmly protested having the wedding in West Monroe. Like Ruth in the bible, she decided her husband's land would be hers too. "No!" she told them. "No, I'm getting married at Temple Baptist because that's where I met Joe at the altar and that's where I'm going raise my family. These roots are firmly planted in the soil. We're not moving. So that's where I'm going to dedicate my children." The Temple church family adopted her in college and Ruston was to be her home.

On August 12, 1978 Joe and Cynthia put down their roots firmly in the peach orchard. It was one of the busiest peach harvest days of the year. Everyone barely made it to the wedding and Joe had been so busy in the shed he came without getting his hair cut.

Ron Cocdy

10

Hanging Out in the Orchard

Moving into the Mitcham Peach Family required big adjustments for the new family member. Cynthia's mother had taken her family to church when they were young but then they bought a camp at D'Arbonne. Her father built a cabin and her mother felt that her loyalty to her husband meant staying right beside him, even on Sunday. A workaholic with a bad temper, her father instilled a certain insecurity in her. As a new member of the peach family her background often kept her from feeling confident around Mr. Mitcham's strong personality.

J.E.'s mother more than made up for his strict personality. Valarie. Everyone loved her and she loved everyone. J.E.'s sweet natured mother grafted Cynthia into the peach family. She was a very strong Christian lady who was very active in their church. She hosted people at her home, putting them in antique beds and rooms that resembled an elegant old plantation house. She would cook and cook and cook until the whole table was full, the kitchen was full and the counters were full. Her friendliness bubbled over. She had a swing in her front yard — very romantic for the new bride--a barn and a farm yard full to the brim with little guineas and chickens and cats.

After marrying, Joe and Cynthia moved into the garden house and renovated it again and again many times over. It became the main house and expanded. They added an open car garage that Joe would eventually close and make into a gun room where he did reloading and sold guns.

The home renovations brought unpleasant surprises on occasion. One day the builders came without announcing their arrival. Cynthia had just finished her finals at Northeast Louisiana University and was exhausted. All of a sudden she was jolted. BAM! She jerked upright, thinking an airplane had hit the house. Outside their house a building crew was knocking off brick with their sledge hammers.

Some days later she went into work and returned home in the rain to find water pouring through a hole in the roof on their sectional sofa. Someone had forgotten to cover it. At least the sofa was somewhat water proof. She urgently called Joe. "Hurry and get home, the rain is coming through the roof like an elephant tee-teeing and I don't know how to contain it. I don't even have a pot, so bring down some tarps from the shed."

She was not happy with the period of renovating but the antics did not stop. One of the builders had cataracts and was blind. Sometimes she even had to go out and measure the lumber for the builders. The cement guys poured the carport slab too high that it blocked the door from opening. Joe got so upset that the door would not open he took a sledge hammer and tried to break up the concrete. It backfired and broke his shin.

The bigger farm house made room for the births of Joe and Cynthia's two girls. Laura and Sarah joined the Ruston peach family and from earliest days learned to enjoy the summer fun under the trees and down by the ponds.

"If you throw your bait in, it makes a plop sound," Cynthia said, expertly describing pond life. "You'll notice that all the brim come. My mother always told me to be quiet when you're fishing." It is good advice and sometimes she has had to remind Joe to lower his voice when he's talking on the cell phone while they are fishing. "Joe talks real loud because he's deaf."

The plopping sound doesn't just grab the breams' attention. There was the time turtles chased the girls. Loggerheads can get quite big with high ridges on their back. When they top the water the ridges lining their shell tops rise up and look almost prehistoric. Sometimes they can be seen around the orchard slowly clawing their way across a road.

When the girls were about 9 and 5, these frightening critters came up and chased the girls, frightening them out of the water. Cynthia paddled to the opposite side of the pond on her air mattress to draw them away from Sarah and Laura. She got close to a shallow area near the water filters, a place they liked to call 'turtle bay.' The water there is shallow and attracts turtles of all sizes. As she paddled away the loggerheads followed along, sticking their heads up like lazy Loch Ness monsters.

When the girls were little they all became so familiar with the turtles that they named them. The one that liked to follow Cynthia they called Chocolate Face. The imaginative girls liked to read books, so they started naming animals on the farm after characters in their books. They called their pet geese Queen Elizabeth and King Edward.

Swimming with turtles may sound odd, but man and beast got used to one another. Mostly. It could still be scary when one especially big one would slowly bob up from the depths next to the raft and there was a full two feet distance between the ridges on the back and the scaly tale sticking up from the water. At that range it could spook even Cynthia, regardless of the cute pet names. Sometimes she would nap on the air mattress and then open her eyes to discover a big turtle head just inches away. After the initial shock wore off she would remind herself, "Everything is beautiful in its own way. I love nature! I collected turtles when I was young."

Each year the loggerheads in Louisiana migrate across the yards and roads. With a half dozen ponds and lakes, the Mitcham Orchard has dozens of turtles in the springtime wandering around in search of a place to bury their eggs. Some always wind up in Joe and Cynthia's yard patiently digging their way under the ornamental bushes to lay their eggs.

While Joe Jr. tended to the peach trees, Cynthia and the girls went treasure hunting. There was an old home place near the orchard. Huge vines and limbs covered the ghost house. They dug up all kinds of interesting things, some of value and others not, like broken commodes. Sometimes they found tiny humming bird nests in the peach trees. Digging in the flower beds they found an old spoon and a gold ring missing its diamond.

Long before the orchard and old ghostly home-places, the orchard lands were rich hunting grounds for Native Americans. The Mitchams found treasures of a different sort down on the Wilder property: lots of arrowheads, pottery and a spearhead. While the girls were deliberate in their treasure hunting, Joe and the workers had too much else happening. They did not spend time looking for artifacts. If they found something it was usually by stumbling upon it while plowing or spraying the trees.

Laura and Sarah, like their father, learned at a young age to work on the orchard. Marzee, known by her grandchildren as 'Grandmother' or 'Grams', took care of the girls after school and much of the time in the summer. They called Mr. Mitcham 'Granddaddy'. He enjoyed time with the girls, though he was not a warm, cuddly person. They noticed that even after he retired he would still come around the peach shed and tell the teenagers not to talk too much or not to leave their soda cans laying around.

J.E. liked to have the girls at the family dinner table. He always sat at the head of the table. Sarah was hesitant to talk in front of him because she did not feel confident of her grammar. Laura felt like her grammar was pretty good, so she would speak up sometimes. If anyone did ever slip up, J.E. was sure to correct them; that is, if he actually heard them. His hearing was terrible and he would not wear his hearing aids. He wanted everyone to speak up and enunciate. He told them to enunciate like Katie Couric. They tried to protest that the difference was not their enunciation but that he could turn Katie Couric's volume all the way up.

J.E. hated losing his hearing. It particularly bothered him when a couple of people at the other end of the table or room were having a conversation that he could not understand or join. He badly wanted to be included, so he asked them to talk loud enough.

J.E. often asked the girls about their grades in school. He was proud of the fact they had good grades and he urged them to study hard. He was impressed Laura studied Spanish. Sarah loved playing outside and did not ever want to come in from the orchard. The girls enjoyed making up their own plays and acting in their own theaters outside under the trees. As an adult Sarah never lost her dream of getting married in the orchard and holding the reception in the peach shed.

One of J.E.'s favorite things was telling the girls his childhood stories, like things he was proud of from his school days. He remembered going to literary rally in French. Into old age he retained a couple of words and phrases in French. But he was always upset that the person who beat him in the rally was a native French speaker. He thought it simply unfair that she had been allowed to compete against him, a native English speaker from Summerfield in North Louisiana.

For their favorite dessert treat, Marzee made peach cobbler, never peach pie. Occasionally she baked a peach cake or sometimes just cut up a peach and served it over ice cream. But peach cobbler was the main thing their family cherished, in spite of her using margarine instead of real butter.

Another way J.E. enjoyed his peaches was in peach preserves. Marzee made two different kinds, traditional preserves and the other with Indian peaches including the pits. Using her special recipe she cooked them down with cloves and other spices. She said the pit gave it more flavor.

No peach was free, even for Marzee. She only used peaches that were leftover or had fallen on the ground. Sometimes she walked over to the shed and got the cheapest culls that would not sell. Other times she went behind the house with a little orange plastic bucket and gather peaches off the ground. She never thought of cutting up a perfect, beautiful peach that the family could sell.

Peaches can ferment, but the Mitchams never made peach wine. J.E. and Marzee were hardcore Baptists. The girls only saw J.E. drink alcohol once or twice. On New Year's Eve 1999 their cousin brought over some champagne to celebrate. Everyone tried a few sips but they unanimously decided it was disgusting.

During the peach festival, back when there were several peach orchards in town, the different growers held competitions for different categories of peach. They tried to win with the sweetest peach, best looking peach, biggest peach or smoothest peach, which seemed a bit silly since they could simply knock the fuzz off by running them through the bristled rollers of their machines. On the morning of the competition Marzee rose early and went through the peach shed, sorting through the ones she wanted to take. Over the years the competitors decreased with the closing of peach orchards until almost no one was left, giving Marzee an easy win. That did not lesson her enjoyment of the little plaques she took home summer after summer.

The Mitcham ladies always enjoyed going to the arts and crafts fair but J.E. and Joe never had time for festival fun. The Ruston Peach Festival continues each summer, drawing huge crowds. In 2015 the Hampton Inn sponsored an earth shaking 2,251 pound peach cobbler, earning a place in the Guinness Book of World Records. It had "819 lbs of peaches, 312 lbs of butter, 343 lbs of flour, 73 gallons of milk, 1 lb of baking powder, 454 lbs sugar, and took 6 hours to cook"[2]. J.E. would have been very pleased to see that they used butter and not margarine.

Marzee took her own vacations because J.E. never left ~~the farm.   She mostly tra~~veled with the church on

[2]
http://www.worldrecordacademy.com/food/largest_peach_cobbler_Lou isiana_Peach_Festival_breaks_Guinness_World_Records_record_2153 82.html

trips organized by Dale Oden or her sister from Texas. Sometimes Joe Jr. would drive the church bus since he had a chauffer's license. Marzee's kitchen had a large wooden display cut in the shape of the US that displayed her collection of spoons from every state in the country. After she died her family started finding cans and old baby food jars filled with pretty little rocks, seashells and colorful stones. It took them many hours of puzzling over the collections before they figured out that Marzee had kept them as mementoes from her travels in the US and outside in England, Canada, Mexico and Haiti. The youngest of seven kids and raised in the Great Depression, she was always frugal. On one daring occasion she visited a casino in Las Vegas and slipped a coin in a slot machine. She did not bother to ever tell J.E.

One year Cynthia and Joe entered Laura in the Princess Peach pageant. Riding into town from the virtual jungle of peach trees, the bright little five year old imagined how she would look in her new crown. Victory seemed inevitable, just like Gram Marzee bringing home those plaques year after year. She had to win she thought, because without her family they would not be having a peach festival.

But she did not win. None of the Mitcham family members ever won. People came from anywhere. Hopeful parents and grandparents put their little girls in the pageant. They did not have to sing or perform, just look cute and the competition was always stiff.

In the early years of the orchard J.E. never held a party or celebration to mark the close of the season. In later years Joe Jr. liked to organize a 4th of July bar-b-ques, even though it came at a very busy time. More retirees had started working in those days. Some enjoyed putting their culinary skills to work so they grilled and basted for everyone's enjoyment.

In a very generous show of appreciation for the Ruston Peach Family, people from across the US regularly sent gifts to the orchard. The Mitchams received fresh fruits, vegetables, steaks, sausages, stuffed chickens, shrimp, crawfish and watermelons. They especially enjoyed slicing the watermelons on Friday afternoon when everyone was gone and the work was finished.   It seemed that the neighborly gestures came because peach lovers everywhere wanted to give back a part of what was important to them from their own lives.

11

Frozen Peaches

The Mitchams, like the whole Ruston community, could never forget the drama and uncertainty of the early spring freezes. In a matter of hours a cold front could kill the tiny peach blossoms and bring financial ruination. As temps fell Rustonites saw the urgent need and generously came to the orchard to help. They put every resource to use. Burning tires scattered by the dozens throughout the orchard staved off the freezing temperatures. At other times they burned coal. Men stayed up all night tending the fires while the women helped out by making sandwiches and coffee. During their breaks, the exhausted men came in from the fields with smoke and soot on their faces. They kept the fires burning in the orchard through the night.

A few times the Mitchams hired a helicopter to circle a couple of hundred feet above the orchard to push the warm air down, desperate for any way to save some of the crop. In later years Joe installed more than a dozen huge wind machines at strategic points throughout the orchard. They would stir up the air just enough to stop a freeze. Sometimes a freeze came multiple times in one year but usually only once.

The first devastating freeze came in 1955, the same year Joe was born. The next freeze fell in 1986, the year Sarah was born. There was no complete freeze in between 1955 and 1986, but then they had seven years in a row. Almost every tree was affected. One year it only took a few hours to gather the 'harvest'. J.E. and Marzee, being strictly honest, said that yes, they had sold something here or there, like a gift box, so the crop insurance would not cover the losses.

On some years they did not need to open the shed. One time Joe only hired a handful of pickers and put Laura to work in the fields with them. She rode in a wagon behind the tractor. The pickers hauled over the boxes of peaches so she could transfer them into the boxes to be sold. In the afternoon Laura sat in J.E. and Marzee's driveway selling peaches. She laughed when old men came by and thought she was a boy since she had her hair up in a baseball cap.

Hail also destroyed the peach crop. A bad hail storm hit one spring and Joe could only hire a few people to work under the shed. There were a couple of retired ladies, Laura and three or four of her friends. They did everything by hand that year. The hail had damaged the peaches, making deep gouges where bacteria and fungi grew. In the high heat the disease grew quickly so by the time they picked them they were rotten. The Mitchams threw away incredible amounts of fruit, including ruined nectarines and plums. A local hog farmer came by each day and took barrel after barrel of the stinking, rotten fruit.

Hail and freeze took their toll on the Ruston peach industry. At one point in the 70s and 80s, between the Mitchams, Owens, Summeralls, Lawrences and Hollises, there was over 1000 acres of peaches in Lincoln parish. With 360 acres Mr. Owens had more land than the Mitchams, but the Mitcham orchards produced more peaches because of land management and farming techniques. The 80s freezes decreased the number of growers and acres in Lincoln Parish. Mr. Owens passed away in 1985; eventually, the freezes of 86, 87 and 89 had put his family orchard out of business.

2

Loving Labor

All the Mitchams pitched in on the farm. As a little girl Laura sat next to her Daddy on a bench and helped grade the peaches and sort them out. Around 12 years old she started packing them and at 15 years old started selling the peaches. By the time she attended college she had tired of working on the farm.

When Sarah was little she sat on the table with Joe and helped him count out his money. She took over the store during the summer and came up with all sorts of marketing plans. Sarah wrote 2 cookbooks.

One season a local new article commented about the Mitcham Peach Orchard being a million dollar industry. Some of the public misinterpreted the article to mean millions of dollars of profit. The girls sometimes felt that people thought they were from a well-to-do family, but the truth was that the business did not net that much money. The cost of running the farm on a good year with its employees, equipment and countless other expenses did not leave much extra.

"People can get very rude about fruit." The family has seen some tense moments during peak season. Laura comments, "They act like it's a lot more important than it is. Some people drove a long way and waited a long time and got hot, but our family and workers were hot, too." People showed up wanting peaches and could not get them. Lots of times the Mitchams had to put a limit on the purchases. A long line of customers wrapped around the shed. The sales people explained to them that they could buy only such and such an amount in order to try to stretch out the peaches so everyone could get a little.

Once or twice a year Joe Jr., normally known as a laid-back sort of guy, would have a bad day. Everything went wrong—pickers picked fruit either too firm or too ripe and sometimes the dumper broke down. Joe preferred running the machinery and supervising the whole operation so it ran smoothly. Usually he left the customer relations to someone else. But sometimes a customer thought he deserved special treatment. One time a customer refused to wait in line and started bugging Joe. In rare moments Joe would reach the end of his patience with the pesky complainer.

Sometimes the workers got out of hand. One afternoon a silly 15 year old girl was working on the line grading peaches. She kept loudly singing annoying songs like 'This is the Song that Never Ends'. It was too much and Joe started yelling at her and fired her.

There were the boys who were supposed to be stapling boxes. They were not working and just sitting around taking it easy. Joe caught them smoking, which was the ultimate no-no in the shed. Joe could vividly remember the scenes of the first shed going down in flames. They got sent away pronto.

On the Mitcham farm hiring was always a seasonal affair. There were retired ladies working on the grading lines. Teenagers and college students packed the peaches. A separate crew worked the fields. In the late 80s and early 90s OSHA started requiring workers to wear pants and long tee-shirts to protect them from the itchiness of the peach fuzz and the effects of sprays.

Freebee give-ways always lightened the mood. One year a gourmet cookbook featured the Mitcham peaches with a photo of Joe. The recipe used peaches in a dish similar to Bananas Foster. It used peaches cooked with cinnamon, something like rum and butter, flambéed and served over ice cream. The peach orchard market sold the recipe packet as make-it-yourself seasoning. Joe enjoyed mingling with the customers and passing out samples of ice cream.

Some peach lovers overestimated their health benefits. When working in the local hospital, Cynthia saw diabetics come in with a blood sugar count of 800-1000 when it should have been 100. The doctors asked about their diet. "I don't understand," they would say, "my diet's great; I've been going to the orchard every day and eating my peaches." Some were eating 10 peaches a day!

With hundreds of teens working at the orchard over the years, romances were bound to happen. One year all the girls got a crush on a Tech guy from Oak Grove. Laura was only 12 at the time and he was a freshman at Tech. She fell in love briefly. He was a genuinely friendly guy who could actually talk to girls of all ages. No doubt it was not the first or last summer peach romance, real or imagined.

13

The Long Let-go

Cynthia worried about J.E. every evening. He was getting much older and feebler. Joe always assured her that his daddy would come in from the fields. Cynthia kept track of him in the fields by watching him pruning the trees across from their house. On many nights J.E. would be the only one still in the fields pruning the baby trees all alone.

All his farming days, J.E. regularly and gladly loaned workers money if they had a need of any kind. He never suspected people of drugs when they came asking for money. He did not ask many questions and did not wait around for them to pay him back. On one occasion he helped an employee cover travel expenses to a recovery program in another city.

One evening some of the guys went out to borrow money from him, but they unexpectedly found him slumped under a tree unconscious. In a panic the workers put him in a truck and rushed to get Joe and Cynthia. An O.R. nurse by profession, she started recognized stroke symptoms and started giving quick instructions. J.E. started to come to at one point, mumbling softly. "I don't want to go to the hospital." He looked around at Joe and repeated, "you're not taking me to the hospital." Joe turned into the Hollis driveway a mile down the road. J.E. kept saying, "don't take me." It became an argument between the nurse, son and father about turning around. Joe always did what his father said and never rebelled. But this was different. They drove back onto the road and got J.E. to the hospital.

Among other things J.E. had dehydrated while working. His workers normally kept water coolers in the trucks, but Mr. Mitcham never took water with him. He drank lots of tea with his meals and took water from the coolers in the workers' trucks.

The doctors wanted to admit him to the hospital. He slowly got better, but the work and pressure never let up. J.E. had passed down his pruning technique to Joe Jr. and a worker named Becky, a sister of Joe's good friend and highly dependable field manager Steve. She worked as a secretary and ran the store and J.E. invited her to work along beside him, even though he always felt that he was the only one who could prune the brand new, little trees when they first went into the soil.

One of J.E.'s best friends was O.O. Osburn and his wife Louise. They called him 'Chief' for short, since he used to be chief of police for Ruston. People often confused Chief and J.E. Every summer the Osburns drove into the orchard with their camper trailer and hooked up in the shed near the loading dock. They moved in for the whole season, running the dumper, helping with jobs and selling peaches.

Chief bought some land where he and his wife hoped to build a house in their later years. One day he was working on the land, watering trees and clearing underbrush. The details are not exactly clear, but he must have had a heart attack while he was tending to a brush fire. Someone called in a fire and his son, who was working that day in the police department, was the first to recognize the address and rush to

help. Sadly they found that the fire had taken his life.

Something seemed to change in J.E. when he lost his friend Chief. He started backing off more and more from the farm work. His

Mr. J. E. Mitcham, Sr.

memory was not as good and he was getting more irritable with the people. He let Joe have even more responsibility for the operations. Chief had been such an important part of J.E.'s life...one of his best friends. His personality was opposite the task-oriented personality of J.E. Chief was warming and engaging. He would light up when a friend drove up. He made everyone feel loved with a big hug. When Laura and Sarah visited the shed Chief and Louise hugged them and showered them with little barrettes, bows, necklaces and plastic jewelry. Although they had grandkids of their own who lived in town, they always treated the Mitcham girls like their own.

It seemed strange to the family when J.E. started giving Joe more responsibility and letting him run the shed. They had some disagreements about what to do in the fields. Joe wanted to invest money in the irrigation system and his father did not want to. They were both visionaries, but Mr. Mitcham did not want to replace the equipment; except for tractors, which J.E. replaced more frequently than Joe.

As J.E. got older he called Joe more and more. Like when he remembered something and wanted to tell Joe just then before forgetting. The calling became constant whenever Joe left the shed. Sometimes he did not want Joe to leave at all.

As he took on more leadership of the orchard, Joe Jr. talked his father into increasing peach quality and profit with less land. Every day in 1973 the orchard sent out an 18-wheeler loaded with 1400 boxes of peaches to supermarkets in Houston and other cities. While the wholesale market meant massive sales it yielded small profits.

Under Joe's plan, the orchard grew in new directions. James Davison ran a big trucking company and was one of the first millionaires in Ruston. He bought Mitcham peaches and sent gift boxes to governors and presidents. Shady Wall, a West Monroe banker, purchased gift boxes for clients. Joe's suggestion of shifting to the retail market worked well. They reduced the acreage, invested in a higher quality underground irrigation system and starting retailing their peaches. The orchard produced larger and tastier peaches while increasing profits.

All those years Marzee did the orchard accounting. She was a school teacher too, so she kept busy in the evenings with the farm work and had more time for book-keeping in the summer months. Her family thought her book-keeping system was strange, perhaps another sign of having grown up in the Great Depression. She had her own particular way of making bank deposits and she did not believe in putting all the money in the same bank. When Joe took on more of the family business, he came to his mother at some point in the 1990s. He pointed to piles of boxes in the back office and said, "You know, you really don't have to keep these records all the way back to the 50s. If we get audited they probably won't need those." They shifted their accounting into new technology, using computer data systems.

J.E.'s health gradually went down. When he was in ICU on another occasion the doctor gave him a sedative with an odd side-effect. It made J.E. talk 72 hours straight. All that time he wanted Joe standing right beside his hospital bed. Joe was always his right-hand man.   Under the influence of the medication J.E. talked on and on as though hallucinating.   He gave work instructions to Joe. Some of the time J.E. interviewed imaginary workers from the past, such as the kids that he hired in the summer. He told them to line up and then gave them his spiel about needing to be at the shed at such and such a time, getting there fifteen minutes before work to find out when they had to come in on the next day. He said, "We'll tell you the day before so ya'll listen, when we quit for the day we will tell you about the next day or you may get a phone call."   Then he would say something like, "Linda, quit squirming and listen up." He passed out assignments, telling Joe to go plow a field or go do a certain chore. He was hallucinating, but accurately hired people, pruned and worked in the fields. He talked so long that his voice went hoarse. The family finally convinced the doctors to change his medication. Running the orchard was his life. He ran it even while semi-conscious.

14

Farm hazards

Even during off months the farm has a lot of pruning and planting new trees, laying down irrigation lines and maintaining them, but work does slowdown in the winter. Joe Jr. loved having extra time to do anything that involved a bulldozer and backhoe, pushing around dirt. Over the years he has expanded and dug out dams for several of the ponds on the farm.

The Mitcham ponds provide essential water to irrigate the orchard, not just giving a home to fish and loggerheads. On one occasion Joe had to dig out an irrigation pond. He pushed over a medium size tree and suddenly saw something odd. Covered in roots from the tree, a rolled-up, clear vinyl tarp was buried under the tree. He hopped down for a closer look. It was large, almost as large as a human. A chill creeped up his spin. He cautiously pulled it open, exposing black hair and a skeleton. This was too much. He called his dad. Did he know anything about a dog or something buried under a tree on the dam? He was nervous. This did not seem right. Perhaps he should call the sheriff. After further examination they came to a conclusion. Someone years earlier had buried a big dog in the orchard by wrapping it in a plastic bag. Either they never told the Mitchams or they simply forgot it. It was a big piece of land and they could not know everything that happened on it over the years.

On July 28, 2005 a real tragedy struck. Augustine Obein worked for the Mitcham family at least ten years. He was from a small village deep in the countryside of Nigeria. He had ritual scarification on his face and spoke with a strong accent. Earning many degrees from Grambling, Augustine stayed in Ruston a long time. He worked for Joe and did lots of other odd jobs around town during the off season. He had a family locally. A cheerful and friendly guy, Augustine enjoyed the Mitchams and became a family friend.

One day after work all the workers gathered out by the upper pond. Someone bet Augustine he could not swim all the way across. He was probably aware that the pond had previously been very shallow and Joe had dug it out. It did not matter. Though he could not swim he took the bet. Money was no problem for him. He had a large amount of cash in his pocket that he pulled out and handed to someone. He went into the water, going deeper and deeper. He tried to swim across, getting farther from the shore. The people on the side watched in horror as he sank. The Mitchams had to call the sheriff department to bring in divers to recover the body.

Something about the curves and hills of Mitcham Orchard Road can make drivers get a heavy foot on the gas pedal. Over the years the orchard has seen many car wrecks. Down the hill from Joe and Cynthia's house an old bridge and sharp curve often proved too difficult for drivers to maneuver. Many people landed in the field next to it. The workers knew that Cynthia had emergency care training so they would come to her first to help people in the wrecks.

Thirty years ago there was much less traffic of the four-wheel kind on Mitcham Orchard Road. There was a problem however with the four-legged kind. Sometimes a huge herd of escaped cattle used to roam around the orchard.

Cynthia tried to avoid the cattle on her exercise runs, but it was not always possible. One day someone staked a huge bull in the orchard near her running path. As usual, she ran up and down the road in and around the orchard. She came around a corner with her little poodle that always ran with her, and abruptly stood face to face with the massive, drooling bull. She stopped in her tracks. Up the hill in the peach shed Joe and his buddies were watching her with binoculars, guffawing at the sight of Cynthia, the poodle and bull. No one could exactly say which one was more surprised.

15

Armillaria Attack

Calhoun used to be home for the LSU peach experiment station. Any time the Mitchams needed help with a question about a chemical, a new product on the market, spray programs, or weed control, they could call the Calhoun station. Since J.E. planted the first peach trees in 1947 the Calhoun station worked closely with him and other growers to breed and develop several varieties like Ouachita Gold, Ruston Red, Harvester, La Jewel, and Number 72. When the Mitchams cultivated 340 acres of peaches they had at one time 32 varieties of peaches. They now grow 18.

John Albert's old hog pen gave the Mitcham orchard one of its most special variety of peaches. Almost like magic, the Ruston Red popped out on a tree just below Joe and Cynthia's house near the hog pen. One year, J.E. and Joe noticed a peach tree growing there with a limb called a sport bud. The sport bud is an odd, naturally occurring unique variety that appears on a tree. Farmers can manipulate a tree with grafting, but a sport bud is a natural limb with a new variety that forms on the tree. The tree by the hog pen created a really good looking peach, so the Mitchams kept their eye on it for several years and got cuttings off of it.

Thus the Ruston Red was born. It made an excellent peach. The perfect peach is hard to find. It takes special size, color, firmness, flavor and disease resistance. The Ruston Red had most of those characteristics. The one fault it had was just before it gets ripe the fruit starts falling off the tree. The juicy peaches literally grow themselves off their stem because of its weakness.

Growers around the US recognize the name Ruston Red. Unfortunately, perhaps because of genetics or cutting the buds over the years it has become less red and more yellow.

The Ruston Red was a gift of nature…and John Albert's hog pen. Throughout their career the Mitchams never experimented with artificial pollination or cross-breeding on the orchard. On a couple of occasions they tried grafting but never with any success because of local climate problems.

The Louisiana climate contributed to the Mitchams' most deadly enemy. Until the 1990s the Mitchams won the war against the dark specter growing invisibly on the roots of oak trees. *Armillaria mellea,* sometimes called oak root fungus or honey fungus, can live on the roots of healthy oak trees without causing disease. The Louisiana creek bottoms are probably full of Armillaria, especially in a climate of regular and abundant rain, plenty of heat and high temperatures.

J.E. knew about this nemesis from the beginning of the orchard. When planting a new peach sapling, they had a simple system for preparing the soil to

protect against the fungus. First they buried a can of methyl bromide, a poisonous gas that would effectively sterilize the soil from Armillaria. The can was air-tight and since it was poisonous, they had to release it underground. Next they covered it thoroughly with soil and placed the point of a long, spear-like tool on the can. When it was completely covered, they plunged the spear point into the can, releasing the methyl bromide gas underground. The Mitchams repeated this process 10,000 times. Burying, piercing, releasing and sterilizing the soil. Every peach sapling had to have a can of methyl bromide gas released if it would survive honey fungus attack.

Until 1995 this system worked well and the orchard produced tons of peaches, as long as the hail and freezes did not get them. But then the Environmental Protection Agency regulated methyl bromide. Citing destruction to the ozone layer, the EPA and other environmental organizations worldwide sought to end it usage.

Without methyl bromide or any substitute, new trees had to be planted without protection from oak tree fungus. From 2000 onward the Mitchams watched their trees turn yellow and brittle. Mushrooms started popping up around the bases of the trees.

Death and disease spread across the hills until the orchard went from 10,000 peach trees to about 1500.

The national news media got wind of the looming disaster. Reporters showed up on the farm with their questions. Why is the orchard dying? Can you find a substitute for methyl bromide? What are your plans for the future? Joe patiently explained that there was nothing he could do. Along with the rest of Ruston and the nation, he watched the orchard start to slowly fade away.

News of the fungus attack brought many well-meaning suggestions. Joe got calls from all kinds of companies wanting to sell him their product, assuring him that this time it would solve the problem. Two or three sounded promising and one made the tree heathier with sweeter fruit, but still the fungus spread from root to root at the same rate. Perhaps if he had started with some of the new fungicides when the tree was just a sapling it might have made a real difference. But with trees already ten years old and older, it seemed to be too little, too late.

Getting closer to retirement age, Joe decided to view the loss in a new light. The numbers and the profit became less, but Joe could continue to produce peaches in a way more friendly to the natural land that he had lived on all his life.

Into his 90s, J.E. watched the orchard lose the battle against the fungus. When he reached 92 years of age he continually had trouble falling out of bed. While the remaining peach trees across the hills started to display their beautiful pink blooms in March 2010, he came to the end of his days. J.E. passed away quietly in his farm house.

Marzee lived another three years. She vowed she would never go to a nursing home as long as she could open a can of tomato soup. She managed to open those soup cans for a couple of years. Eventually dementia required a move to the nursing home. A stoke claimed her life in 2013. Trusting in her savior Jesus Christ, she passed into heaven to join her faithful husband J.E.

16

The New Peach Market

Undaunted by the fungus, Joe envisioned a new way to bring life into the Mitcham Orchards. In 1999 he joined with two area fruit processors to create a wide range of products using over-ripe and peaches left-over in harvest season. The Mitchams built a rustic market connected to the steel processing shed, decorated in the summer with dozens of lush ferns hanging along the edge of the roof.

The peach market has become the centerpiece of the new activities of Mitcham Orchards. In early spring they start selling peach ice cream in single or larger quantities. The market has a roomy front porch that overlooks hundreds of acres of peach trees, the expanded ponds and lakes and the dark green forests the stand on the edge of the orchard. Workers keep the orchard tidy with regular mowing and trimming, making it a very popular place for photography, artwork and simply stopping for a restful view in one of north Louisiana's most scenic havens.

The peach market expanded its product line in the 2000s, filling the shelves of the store with a delicious array of fruit preserves and jellies, pepper jellies, fruit butters, cobblers in a jar, syrups of many flavors, canned fruit, pickled vegetables, relishes, salsas, dips, salad dressings, sweets and candies, freshly made fudges, dessert and drink mixes and attractively packed gift boxes.

JOE MITCHAM, JR.
Mitcham Farms

In May and June the peaches still start rolling in from the fields. In spite of smaller yields, Mitcham Orchard has figured out a way to make the most of every reddish-yellow peach. What used to be a quick afternoon snack enjoyed under a shade tree can now be prepared as fine cuisine to enhance a meal as a salsa or dip, bringing the delicious flavor of Ruston peaches into homes across the country.

17

Job Well Done

If someone had noticed an aged J.E walking in the orchard some lovely summer evening, they might have confused him for one of his own gnarled trees. On those peaceful nights J.E. could view the wide horizon to the east and west. Ruston's water tank stood a few miles to the east. A grove of towering pines and oaks on the orchard's southeast rose up just high enough to block his view of Louisiana Tech's Wyly Tower.

Looking to the west he would pause. Most evenings at Mitcham Orchard, the elements did something very unusual. With the skill of a great artist, the twilight sun, sky and soil conspired as one to dip into their color pallet and recreate the hues of a fat, ripened peach. On the edge of the orchard, the dark forests framed the whole scene, looming up, dark and mysterious. The elements captured the beauty of Ruston's local treasure in its grand act of closing the day. This humble farmer, accomplished teacher, musician, and godly man could both appreciate the gift and the giver.

J.E. probably did not set out to create the Ruston icon. But working over decades to build an industrial orchard and then organic farm, that is exactly what he, his friends and his family did. They gave Ruston a name and an identity.

Unlike Louisiana's old cities, Lincoln Parish and Ruston had no waterways. Monroe and West Monroe sprang up on the Ouachita River and flourished with steamboats. Shreveport became a major trading center on the Red River. Baton Rouge and New Orleans opened to the world with their Mississippi River gateways. Ruston? Well...

Founded after the Civil War as a train depot, Ruston had its rusty rails and nails and whistle-blowing engines. Pushed onto the land, railways do not have natural roots. Trains pass through with travelers and cargo. They make a lot of noise and smoke.

Louisiana Tech sprang up in Ruston in 1894, bringing many generations of students. Students are sort of like trains. They just keep passing through. Ruston needed roots. Ruston needed something that belonged, something in the native soil.

J.E. gave Ruston something it needed. He gave it roots. At the height of the Mitcham Peach Orchard he could walk under the green boughs of 34,000 trees. Each one his own planting. In a strange parallel, the population of Ruston grew like the orchard. 34,000 peach trees, 34,000 people. Young people married, babies came into the world and at the same time new trees took root with fresh crops of peaches warming in the summer sun. J.E.'s orchard helped inspire the community of Ruston to put down roots, grow well and bear good fruit.

The peach. The Ruston Peach Family. Longevity and blessing. Job well done.

Do not be deceived: God is not mocked, for whatever one sows, that will he also reap. For the one who sows to his own flesh will from the flesh reap corruption, but the one who sows to the Spirit will from the Spirit reap eternal life. And let us not grow weary of doing good, for in due season we will reap, if we do not give up.

-- GALATIANS 6:7-9

ABOUT THE AUTHOR

Ron Coody graduated from West Monroe High School in 1982, along with several hundred ambitious Southerners, many of whom have ranged out far and wide across the US and the world since then. In 1986 he graduated from Louisiana Tech with a degree in microbiology. Interested in not only nature but the Source of nature, he earned a Master of Divinity from Anderson School of Theology and later a PhD in Intercultural Studies from Concordia Theological Seminary. Along with his wife Jean and their five sons they have enjoyed eating peaches all along the Silk Road from near the edge of China to Istanbul and Greece.